YOUR KNOWLEDGE HAS VALUE

AF150343

- We will publish your bachelor's and master's thesis, essays and papers

- Your own eBook and book - sold worldwide in all relevant shops

- Earn money with each sale

Upload your text at www.GRIN.com
and publish for free

Bibliographic information published by the German National Library:

The German National Library lists this publication in the National Bibliography; detailed bibliographic data are available on the Internet at http://dnb.dnb.de .

Imprint:

Copyright © 2018 GRIN Verlag
Print and binding: Books on Demand GmbH, Norderstedt Germany
ISBN: 9783346108463

This book at GRIN:

https://www.grin.com/document/517329

Sophie Emilie Beha

How I see current authoritarian political changes in Hungary appearing in people's everyday life

Everyday Life in Socialist Hungary

GRIN Verlag

Eötvös Loránd Tudományegyetem

ELTE Budapest

Faculty of Humanities

How I see current authoritarian

political changes in Hungary

appearing in people's everyday life

Paper in the subject
"Everyday life in Socialist Hungary"

Submitted from: Sophie Emilie Beha

Submitted at: 24.05.2018

Table of contents

1. Introduction

Spending my semester abroad in Hungary is more due to chance than it was a personal decision. Originally I wanted to go to Istanbul in Turkey. In addition to Western culture, one thing that interested me most about this country was the lack of press freedom. I wanted to know what it's like to live in a country where press freedom and freedom of expression are not self-evident. However, at a relatively short notice, a student from the Netherlands was jailed in prison and my university ended its cooperation with Istanbul. There were only a few countries to choose from, one of which was Hungary. And since the situation of freedom of the press and freedom of expression are not exactly the same but similar to Turkey, I decided to spend my semester abroad in Budapest. After living in Budapest for the past few months, I got an insight into daily life in Hungary. During my time here, the elections took place (8.04.2018) and I found myself in the midst of a political change that, of course, also influenced everyday life. In the time period before the election, the country was obviously in a tense atmosphere. Election posters lined every street, every path. Fidesz pens were distributed in the pedestrian zone, Fidesz advertisement was in the mailboxes. No one talked about their own political opinions in the street, but it became visible: at the partys' electoral posts in Budapest, the post of Momentum party at Deak Ferenc Square was almost unremarkable, while the Fidesz or Jobbik posts were well under pressure, or in bars, in left autonomous centers like the Gólya or Auróra, Orbán was mocked, and elsewhere, right-wing people tried to intimidate other-minded people. The elections on 8. April 2018 were a great victory for Viktor Orbán and the Fidesz party. Fidesz reached a two-thirds majority, although the opposition has received more votes thanks to the Hungarian electoral system, Viktór Orbán is now in power for a another four years and his policies will of course have an impact on citizens' everyday lives.

On the fallowing pages I will outline the current political situation, define everyday life and then talk about the consequences of change.

2. Current politics in Hungary

Viktor Orbán won the parliamentary elections in Hungary on April 8, 2018. His right-wing national ruling party Fidesz can rule alone in the coming years. It will be his third continuous term in a row. Critics accuse him of dismantling democracy and disrespecting media freedom (PELINKA, 2018). At European level, Orbán is positioning himself as an opponent of migration, which rejects EU binding quotas for accepting asylum seekers. Orbán says that Hungary's democracy does not have to be "liberal". After he got criticized by the EU Parliament for this point of view, he rowed back to using the term "old-fashioned" – which proves to be only another term for the same thing. Again and again he finds praising words for rulers like Putin and Erdoğan. The Prime Minister is fighting against any deepening influence of the European Union. If the majority of EU countries decide to sanction Poland, Hungary will eventually block them (PELINKA, 2018). According to Mr. Traubner (2018) from The Economist, "the fallout among Hungary's fractured opposition is likely to continue. They failed to focus on a consistent message". Several small liberal or left-wing parties insisted on running their own slates in local constituencies where the failure to reach consensus on a single anti-government candidate cost it numerous seats (TRAUBNER, 2018). Orbán's victory will cause dismay in Brussels, where he is regarded as a difficult customer, but was widely welcomed by nationalist and populist leaders across Europe. Furthermore, his tactics will now be copied by populists elsewhere, as Geert Wilders of the Dutch Party for Freedom already tweeted that the result was "a well deserved victory".

3. Definition of Sociologies of everyday life

According to the Dictionary of Sociology the Sociologies of everyday life are defined as following: "The branches of sociology that investigate the organization and meaning of everyday life, usually (but not exclusively) identified with microsociology and with qualitative research into everyday experiences as diverse as pedestrian behaviour, sleep, telephones, work experiences, talk, and time" (LYNSKEY, 1998).

4. Activism

After the election tens of thousands of people protested the Prime Minister Viktor Orbán and his right-wing national government (in Budapest). Among other things, the participants demanded that the votes of the parliamentary elections should be recalculated, the right to vote be changed and the freedom of the press be secured. Under the slogan "We are the majority", the demonstrators ran through the city center to the parliament. Viktor Gyetai, organizer of one of the demonstrations, said: "We want to live in a constitutional state. We want to live in a true democracy" (ZEIT ONLINE, 2018). Weekly people are going out on the street to protest against the government, those who don't live in Budapest travel to the capital to participate. This marks a change in people's everyday life. "In this collective form of participation, political activism is aimed at enriching the individual with new experiences by executing a so-called experience project [...]. Experience-led activism is connected to the anesthetization of everyday life, and also touches on various forms of self-expression in addition to politics, such as art, entertainment, culture and sport. (SZABÒ, 2017)." The most characteristic features of this type of activism are solidarity protests, altruistic actions and culturally rooted means of self-expression. This activism is mostly manifested at locations connected to activist subcultures and other free communal and cultural premises that are not under surveillance by the government or any other authority (POLLETTA, 1999).

5. Migration

After Orbán's election victories in 2010 hundreds of thousands of Hungarians left the country. Most young Hungarians I know want to leave the country. Péther Németh, a young Hungarian, says: "Everybody in my generation wants to move away". Irén Gödri from the Statistics Office in Budapest presented a study in 2017, according to which around 680,000 Hungarians aged 14 and 40 dream of emigration, and 380,000 have concrete plans for doing so (LAUER, 2018). Almost all Hungarians I know have friends or family members abroad. I assume that the wave of migration will not diminish, but rather increase.

6. Rituals

An important focus of Orbán's politics is nationalism. Among other things, the memory of the past and the mediation of the glorious history and identity belong to the care of the national ideas. This maintenance often happens in the form of rituals such as commemoration. "Functionally, rituals are means of addressing change, breaches in the order of everyday life. [… These] rituals are tightly controlled spheres of activity in the everyday life, reinforced through controlled participation and symbolic communication" (CASH, 2011). Political groups make use of rituals and festive peripheries to frame their messages and to increase their symbolic power (KERTZER, 1988; STOELTJE, 1993). Commemorations reveal the discourse of power, mediate messages of memory and identity, and tell us about the communities which generate them. The production of a commemoration can involve many members of a community in a controlled partnership (TURNER, 1968). For Hungary mediation as part of politics, it is shown by commemorations of 15 March 1848, the anniversary of the start of the 1848-49 war of independence (CASH, 2011). At the commemoration of the 15 of March in 2018 I was attending a speech of Orbán. There he spoke of several NGOs, cultural institutions and journalists as enemies. Very shortly after that a newspaper and spokesman of the government, published several black lists with those so called enemies. According to Jens Preissler, Press Secretary of the German Embassy, very shortly after the publication of the black lists, several NGOs received calls and letters in which they were accused of treason. This shows how Orbáns politics as displayed in a commemoration manifests an enemy image and immediately attracts actions who impair people's everyday lifes.

7. Reporting

Hungarians mainly receive their information through TV programs. RTL, TV2 and the state channels are the main sources of information. The government channels and also TV2, since the change of the ownership, broadcast government propaganda. RTL Klub has remained the only independent medium among the largest sources of information. Together with the media law, the government installed its people in the media authority. They assign licenses, punish critical media and impose fines (OSZVÁTH, 2017). Media researcher Ágnes Urbán points out: "There is freedom of the press in the sense that not all media have been closed, there is not this 'party-certain-all-order' as it was before the turnaround, but most media users only have access to a very controlled and manipulated media offer" (VERSECK, 2018). The closure of independent newspapers such as "Népszabadság" and "Magyar Nemzet" was a shock to the population and a slap in the face of press freedom. Now "Lanchid Radio" and "Magyar Narancs" are threatened with closure. Both media companies have already had to cut jobs (GRUSKA, 2018, LEONHARD, 2018). Hungary researcher Vetter even calls press freedom in Hungary "canceled" (VETTER, 2012). This has a big impact on the daily lives of all citizens, because nobody can inform themselves freely anymore. All that remains are state press such as "Magyar Idök" or opposition press. Through the state press Orbán and Fidesz can exercise their power and influence readers. This happens on a private level, Orbán said in his speech against migrants, but for the old-fashioned family, on 15 March. Shortly thereafter, "Magyar Idök" published a blacklist of NGOs and later foreign Hungarian correspondents. It states, that the "slave labor" of these journalists consists in "transmitting the most disgusting lies of the ultraliberal opposition to tens of millions anywhere in the world without any filter" (VERSECK, 2018). Black lists should increase the psychological pressure on unwelcome media. It's not the first blacklist of journalists to appear in Hungary in recent history. For example, the entire editorial board of the Hungarian Investigative Portal "Direkt36" is listed in the "Soros Mercenaries" directory of "Figyelö". Fidesz shows, that it can utilize its power and thus massively influence the values and opinions of the people. The country is becoming increasingly frightened and intimidated. According to Reporters Without Borders (2018), the Hungarian press index ranks 73 out of 108 places worldwide this year. This is a drop by two places and I am afraid that Hungary's press index in the coming years will continue to decline under Orbán. Everyday life with independent journalism is almost impossible in Hungary and over the next four years of Orbán and Fiedez rule the oppositional and independent media companies will either gradually close or will be bought up. Thus everyday life of the people will be further influenced by government press.

8. Radicalization

In my opinion an important consequence of the current political changes is clearly the radicalization of everyday life. In the following I will deal specifically with the growing resentments against foreigners, Gypsies and furthermore with the growing antisemitism and nationalism. Additionally, I will focus on the soccer community.

8. 1 Growing resentment against foreigners

Very shortly after I arrived in Hungary I noticed huge billboards in the streets showing a stream of migrants next to a gigantic fence. Printed on the refugee stream was an oversized stop sign, as it is used in road traffic signs. I learned that these signs were part of a costly propaganda operation launched by the government. According to Lendvai (2018) there are also similar billboards, which are aimed at foreign migrants, saying: "If you come to Hungary, you must not take jobs away from Hungarians!"; "If you come to Hungary, you must respect Hungarian culture!" All of these billboards were in Hungarian, so probably not understandable for a Syrian or Afghanian migrant and mainly meant for native Hungarians. "Yet, what cannot be denied is the reality that this transparent and crude attempt to rouse public opinion against foreign refugees was a great public relations success for the Orbán regime" (LENDVAI, 2018). In his speech to the parliament on 15.03.2018 Orbán rushed against foreigners. Very clearly he said: "We are against migrants". This address to the common we,seems to work. On the weekend of the elections, Zsuzsanna Nagy, a middle-aged woman from Cegléd, spoke out against refugees: "I don't want them in my country, they are wrong here." Another Hungarian woman told me, "if the migrants live here, I can no longer go to the swimming pool". I believe that these resentments and prejudices against refugees will now grow even more. Shama Hatim, a twenty-eight year old woman from Morocco who works in accounting and finance in Budapest, has already experienced xenophobia in her workplace when her boss denied her promotion on the grounds that she was "too brown". Now she is worried about the extension of her visa, which is on the verge. After the elections, the visa applications of two of her Moroccan acquaintances were rejected. This clearly shows how everyday life is changing for Hungarians, as their antipathy towards foreigners grows and for foreigners everyday lives in Hungary are getting harder every day.

8. 2 Growing antiziganism

In Hungary not just foreigners but also the Gypsies suffer from resentment. Meyer (2006) points out that "strategies of ostracism and discrimination against Gypsies will continuously be produced until the [...] Hungarian groups experience significant cultural differences in their everyday life." With the current politics this seems not to happen since Orbán reinforces the ostracism of Gypsies rather than mitigates it. Aversion and contempt of Gypsies can be seen throughout the Hungarian society. Whether it's the double bassist who speaks of stealing and stinking Gypsies who take advantage of the state. Or hijack entire houses and drive out the original inhabitants to live there. Or the 16-year-old student from Budapest, who tells me that the Gypsies are beating up young Hungarians for fun and making use of jobs and social benefits that would rather belong to Hungarians. Meyer (2006) confirms that the Gypsies "struggle tenaciously to live up to the expectations of the [...] society". Therefore, I believe that under the current authoritarian political changes in Hungary the image and resentiments of Gypsies are going to deepen further and further.

8. 3 Growing antisemitism

Four days after the election victory Orbán, the pro-government journal "Figyelö" published a list of 200 people allegedly belonging to the network of US billionaire and philanthropist George Soros under the title "The People of the Speculator". This incitement of the Orbán government against Soros has been going on for years. According to Koltai (2018) the "demonization of Soros marks another step in the regime's evolution. The vulgar hate campaign against him has institutionalized thinly veiled antisemitic language, making it part of everyday life". He continues that Hungary might be exceptional in both open and coded antisemitism shapes in public discourse. "Hungary has a rich antisemitic tradition and many citizens remain susceptible to it. Indeed, the entire Hungarian right has worked to revive this language since 1990, and today it has moved to the level of everyday state discourse" (KOLTAI, 2018). For example if we replace the word "Soros" with "Jews" in the hundreds of statements the government's spokespersons and supporters have made, we find the standard tropes of interwar antisemitism: alien parasites and rootless cosmopolitans conspiring against the nation. If this kind of antisemitism is already that widely accepted and part of Hungarian language in everyday life it will probably grow even more under the new Orbán regime. Perhaps some Orthodox Jews will no longer show their religion so openly in the future. Already some Jews have suffered insults in the Jewish quarter in Budapest. Maybe they would not dare to leave the house with kippah or even could cut off their sideburns in future.

8.4 Radicalization in the example of the football community

According to Bálint Jósa, founder of the "Foundation for subjective values", a NGO from Budapest, which regularly carries out projects against discrimination and racism in Hungarian football, the history of Hungarian football is "above all antisemitism and antiziganism" (NIESSEN, 2016). In the days of socialism in the 1970s, songs about trains to Auschwitz and Gypsy calls in the football stadiums were tolerated. The rulers thought that people needed this valve for their prejudices. So socialism taught that modern people were not nationalist, only to let off hatred for Roma, Jews or other countries in the football stadiums. It was a minority of spectators who sang such songs, but they were very loud. Hungarian football has lost a lot of popularity, with the exception of the Ultras, where fans rarely went to the games, so now they take control of the stadiums and network with right-wing groups. Jobbik, the extreme right-wing party in Hungary, and also the extreme right-wing Hungarian Guard, which is a kind of paramilitary right-wing extremist army, have recruited new members for the Hooligans and Ultras (NIESSEN, 2016). As is known, Viktor Orbán is a great football fan. He built many stadiums and is a close friend of the association. The stadium in his home village Felchut has even more seats than Felchut has residents. According to Bálint Jósa (NIESSEN, 2016), Orbán's campaigns against refugees and illegals have brought a more general form of xenophobia into society and football. For example, foreign players in the stadium are mercilessly booed and the largest Hungarian Ultra website "Ultras Liberi" called for distributing poisoned food to refugees (NIESSEN, 2016). In the future Orbán will continue to spend a lot of money on sports rather than education, especially in football. Based on autocratic systems in the world, he sees the perfect propaganda in it. If people are happy about their football club, it distracts them from ongoing policies. Thus in football xenophobia, antisemitism and antiziganism are growing and everyday football is increasingly shifting into the right-wing extremist scene.

9. Conclusion

In this paper the current political situation in Hungary was described and analyzed. In the following, the changes of everyday life were discussed in detail. Manipulative media systems and suppressed press freedom, growing xenophobia, racism, antisemitism and antiziganism as well as simultaneous nationalism and a wave of emigration determine the country and everyday life. Under Orbán's government, the radicalization in the country will increase and intensify. The fear of the unknown and new will grow, as well as the gripping of all straws that offer simple populist solutions but cannot solve any problems. Above all, there will be less resistance in the future, as Orban proceeds massively and with an iron hand against his opponents. The Hungarian office of Amnesty International had to close and many other NGOs cannot resist the pressure that Orbán is building with the Fidesz party. The educated middle and upper classes and academics are increasingly moving abroad. In the country remain Fidesz followers, the politically displeased and the manipulated. And as shown in this paper the country has already begun to change and will do this even more. What we can do is to look to the future with open eyes and to reflect on occurrences, where they come from and how they arise.

Bibliography

Cash, J. J (2011). Commemoration and Contestation. Comparative Hungarian Cultural Studies. Purdue University Press. 247-250.

Gruska, U (2018). Deutsche Korrespondenten auf Schwarzer Liste. Reporter ohne Grenzen. Access on 10. 05. 2018 via https://www.reporter-ohne-grenzen.de/ungarn/alle-meldung-en/meldung/deutsche-korrespondenten-auf-schwarzer-liste/.

Kertzer, I. D (1988). Ritual, Politics and Power. New Haven: Yale University Press.

Koltai, M (2018). Hungary: The End of Democratic Illusions? The government-sponsored attack on the Central European University represents one more step in the country's authoritarian drift. Jacobin. Access on 10. 05. 2018 via https://www.jacobinmag.com/2017/05/-hungary-central-european-university-george-soros-protests.

Lauer, K (2018). Nicht mehr ihre Heimat. Europastaaten. Ungarn. Wiener Zeitung. Access on 09. 05. 2018 via https://www.wienerzeitung.at/nachrichten/europa/europastaaten/956517_Nicht-mehr-ihre-Heimat.html.

Lendvai, P (2018). Orbán. Hungary's Strongman. Oxford University Press. 34-154.

Leonhard, R (2018). Pressefreiheit in Ungarn unter Druck. Orbán triumphiert, Medien leiden. Taz. Access on 10. 05. 2018 via http://www.taz.de/!5494850/.

Lynskey, B (1998). A Dictionary of Sociology. Oxford University Press. 32.

Meyer, S (2006). Central European Political Science Review.

Quarterly of Central European Political Science Association. University of Michigan. 75.

Niessen, B (2016). Wer ist die „Carpathian Brigade", Ungarns Neonazi-Ultragruppe?. Vice Sports. Access on 16.05.2018 via https://sports.vice.com/de/article/ezynwa/wer-ist-die-carpathian-brigade-ungarns-neonazi-ultragruppe.

Ozsváth, S (2017). Pressefreiheit in Ungarn. Eine Frage der Macht. Deutschlandfunk. Access on 10. 05. 2018 via http://www.deutsch-landfunk.de/pressefreiheit-in-ungarn-eine-frage-der-macht.724.de.html? dram:article_id=379321.

Pelinka, A (2018). Pressefreiheit in Ungarn. Europa wird vier weitere Jahre Orbán ertragen müssen. Die Zeit. Access 09. 05. 2018 via https://www.zeit.de/politik/ausland/2018-03/parlamentswahlen-un-garn-victor-orban-fidesz-demokratie/komplettansicht.

Polletta, F (1999). "Free spaces" in Collective Action. Theory and Society. 1-38.

Reporters Without Borders (2018). Press Index. Hungary. Reporters Without Borders. Access on 10. 05. 2018 via https:/rsf.org/en/hungary.

Stoeltje, B (1993). Power and The Ritual Genres: Western Rodeo. Western Folklore. 135-56.

Szabó, A (2017). The role of irony in the political activism of Hungarian youth. Heinrich Böll Stiftung. Access 09. 05. 2018 via https://www.boell.de/en/2017/05/31/role-irony-political-activism-hungarian-youth.

Traubner, E (2018). Hungary's illiberal prime minister, Viktor Orban, wins landslide. The Economist. Access 09. 05. 2018 via https://www.economist.com/europe/2018/04/09/hungarys-illiberal-prime-minister-viktor-orban-wins-a-landslide.

Turner, V (1968). The Ritual Process. Structure and Anti-Structure. Ithaca: Cornell University Press.

Verseck, K (2018). Schikane gegen Medien in Ungarn. Orbáns schwarze Listen. Spiegel. Access on 10. 05. 2018 via http://www.spiegel.de/politik/ausland/medien-in-ungarn-wie-viktor-orban-journalisten-unterdrueckt-a-1205826.html.

Vetter, R (2012). Hungary. A Portrait. CH. Links Publishing Company. 132.

Zeit Online (2018). Zehntausende demonstrieren gegen Orbán. In Ungarn sind zahlreiche Menschen auf die Straße gegangen, um gegen die Regierung und für Demokratie zu demonstrieren. Sie forderten auch eine Änderung des Wahlrechts. Die Zeit. Access 09. 05. 2018 via https://www.zeit.de/gesellschaft/zeitgeschehen/2018-04/ungarn-viktor-orban-demonstration-budapest.

YOUR KNOWLEDGE HAS VALUE

- We will publish your bachelor's and master's thesis, essays and papers

- Your own eBook and book - sold worldwide in all relevant shops

- Earn money with each sale

Upload your text at www.GRIN.com
and publish for free